Easy Mango Cookbook

50 Delicious Mango Recipes

By
BookSumo Press

Published by
http://www.booksumo.com

Table of Contents

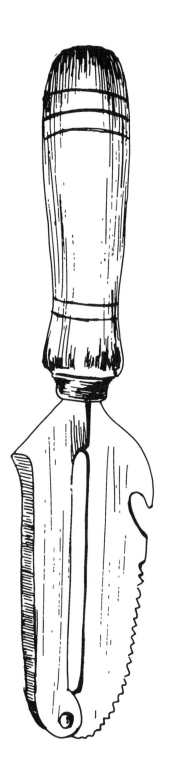

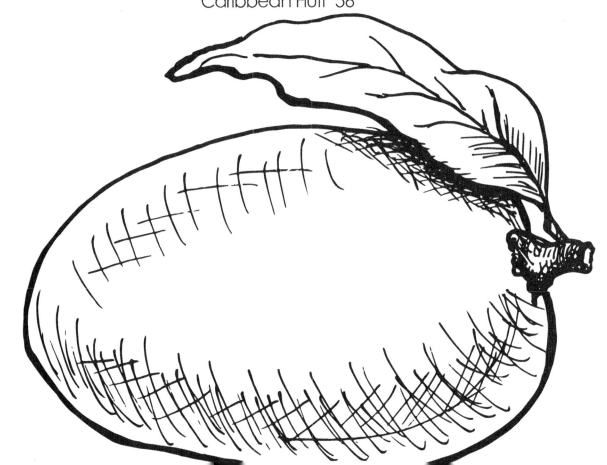

How to Make
Mango Chutney

🥣 Prep Time: 10 mins
🕐 Total Time: 1 hr 40 mins

Servings per Recipe: 20
Calories	46 kcal
Fat	0.2 g
Carbohydrates	11.6g
Protein	0.2 g
Cholesterol	0 mg
Sodium	13 mg

Ingredients

3 C. distilled white vinegar
6 C. white sugar
6 C. brown sugar
1 tsp ground cinnamon
2 tsp ground ginger
4 tsp ground allspice
1 tsp ground cloves
5 small red hot chili peppers, seeded and chopped
1 tsp kosher salt
2 large onions, chopped

3 cloves garlic, chopped
1 C. golden raisins
1 C. raisins
1/2 C. fresh ginger root, chopped
16 C. sliced, semi-ripe mangos
1/2 C. sliced almonds

Directions

1. In a large pan, mix together the chili peppers, vinegar, both the sugars, spices and salt and bring to a boil.
2. Cook for about 30 minutes.
3. Stir in the remaining ingredients except the mangoes and almonds and cook for about 30 minutes.
4. Reduce the heat to low and stir in the mangoes and almonds then simmer for about 30 minutes.
5. Transfer the mixture into the sterilized jars, about 1/2-inch below from the top, then seal tightly.

MANGO TILAPIA
from Guyana

🍲 Prep Time: 10 mins
🕐 Total Time: 22 mins

Servings per Recipe: 4
Calories	319 kcal
Fat	16 g
Carbohydrates	21.2g
Protein	25.3 g
Cholesterol	41 mg
Sodium	562 mg

Ingredients

4 tilapia fillets
2 tbsp olive oil
1 1/2 tbsp grated orange zest
1/4 C. fresh orange juice
salt and pepper to taste
crushed red pepper flakes to taste
Salsa:
1 mango - peeled, seeded and diced
1 small red onion, finely chopped
1 avocado - peeled, pitted and diced

3 roma tomatoes - peeled, seeded and chopped
1 lime, zested and juiced
1 jalapeno pepper, seeded and finely chopped
1 tbsp minced fresh ginger root
1/4 C. chopped fresh cilantro
1 tsp kosher salt

Directions

1. Set your oven to 400 degrees F before doing anything else.
2. In a shallow baking dish mix together the orange zest, oil, orange juice chili flakes, salt and black pepper.
3. Add the tilapia fillets and coat with the mixture generously.
4. Cook everything in the oven for about 10 - 12 minutes.
5. Meanwhile for salsa in a bowl, mix together all the ingredients.
6. Serve the tilapia fillets with a topping of the mango salsa.

Mango Jelly with Saffron

 Prep Time: 15 mins

Total Time: 1 hr

Servings per Recipe: 24

Calories	73 kcal
Fat	0.1 g
Carbohydrates	18.9g
Protein	0.2 g
Cholesterol	0 mg
Sodium	1 mg

Ingredients

2 lb. ripe mangoes
1 1/2 C. white sugar
3/4 C. water

3 saffron threads

Directions

1. Microwave the whole mangoes till soft and keep aside to cool completely.
2. Remove the peel and pit from the mangoes.
3. In a bowl, add the pulp and mash it.
4. In a large pan, mix together the water and sugar on low heat.
5. Bring to a boil, stirring occasionally.
6. Increase the heat to medium-high and boil till the soft threads form.
7. Stir in the mango pulp and saffron threads and boil for about 5 minutes, stirring occasionally.
8. Transfer the jam into sterilized jars and seal according

MONTEGO
Mango Salsa

🥣 Prep Time: 15 mins
🕐 Total Time: 45 mins

Servings per Recipe: 8
Calories	21 kcal
Fat	0.1 g
Cholesterol	5.4g
Sodium	0.3 g
Carbohydrates	0 mg
Protein	1 mg

Ingredients

1 mango - peeled, seeded, and chopped
1/4 C. finely chopped red bell pepper
1 green onion, chopped
2 tbsp chopped cilantro
1 fresh jalapeno chili pepper, finely chopped

2 tbsp lime juice
1 tbsp lemon juice

Directions

1. In a bowl, mix together all the ingredients.
2. Cover and keep aside for about 30 minutes.

Hawaiian
Bread

 Prep Time: 20 mins

 Total Time: 1 hr 30 mins

Servings per Recipe: 16	
Calories	245 kcal
Fat	11.6 g
Carbohydrates	32.9g
Protein	3.4 g
Cholesterol	58 mg
Sodium	312 mg

Ingredients

2 C. all-purpose flour
2 tsp baking soda
2 tsp ground cinnamon
1/2 tsp salt
3 eggs
3/4 C. softened butter

1 1/4 C. white sugar
1 tsp vanilla extract
2 C. chopped mango
1/2 C. shredded coconut
1/4 C. chopped walnuts

Directions

1. Set your oven to 350 degrees F before doing anything else and grease and flour 2 loaf pans.
2. In a bowl, sift together the flour, baking powder, cinnamon and salt.
3. In another bowl, add the eggs, sugar, butter and vanilla and beat well.
4. Fold in the coconut, mango and walnuts.
5. Make a well in the center of the flour mixture.
6. Add the egg mixture into the well of the flour mixture and mix till well combined.
7. Transfer the mixture into the prepared loaf pans and keep aside for about 20 minutes.
8. Cook everything in the oven for about 1 hour.

HOW TO MAKE
Sorbet

🍲 Prep Time: 15 mins
🕐 Total Time: 15 mins

Servings per Recipe: 12
Calories	94 kcal
Fat	0.2 g
Cholesterol	24.6g
Sodium	0.4 g
Carbohydrates	0 mg
Protein	2 mg

Ingredients

4 mangos - peeled, seeded, and cubed
1 C. simple syrup
3 tbsp fresh lime juice

Directions

1. In a food processor, add the mango and pulse till pureed.
2. Add the lime juice and simple syrup and pulse till smooth.
3. Transfer into an ice cream maker and process according to manufacturer's directions.
4. Freeze till set completely.

Creamy
Mango Glazed Sea Bass

Prep Time: 20 mins
Total Time: 40 mins

Servings per Recipe: 4
Calories   423 kcal
Fat   31.1 g
Carbohydrates   13.6 g
Protein   24.2 g
Cholesterol   87 mg
Sodium   222 mg

Ingredients

1/2 mango - peeled, seeded and diced
1/2 C. heavy cream
1 tsp lemon juice
1/2 C. chopped macadamia nuts
1/4 C. seasoned bread crumbs
1 tsp olive oil
1/2 tsp black pepper

1 pinch red pepper flakes
1 lb. fresh sea bass
salt and ground black pepper to taste
2 cloves minced garlic
1 tbsp extra virgin olive oil

Directions

1. Set your oven to 350 degrees F before doing anything else.
2. In a food processor, add the macadamia nuts, bread crumbs, 1 tsp of the olive oil, black pepper, and red pepper flakes and pulse till smooth.
3. For the mango sauce in a small pan, mix together the mango, cream, and lemon juice and bring to a boil. Reduce heat and simmer till mixture becomes thick.
4. Sprinkle the fish with salt and black pepper.
5. In a large skillet, heat 1 tbsp of the oil and garlic on medium heat and sear the fish fillets from the both sides.
6. Now cook the fish in the oven till done completely.
7. Cover the sea bass with macadamia mixture and cook everything in the oven till the crust becomes brown.
8. Serve with a topping of the mango cream sauce.

MANGO
Relish 101

Servings per Recipe: 4

Calories	63 kcal
Fat	1.4 g
Carbohydrates	13.7g
Protein	0.7 g
Cholesterol	0 mg
Sodium	149 mg

Ingredients

1 mango - peeled, seeded and diced
1 tsp extra virgin olive oil
1/2 red bell pepper, chopped
2 green onion, thinly sliced
1 tbsp chopped cilantro
1 lime, juiced

1/4 tsp salt
1 pinch cracked black pepper
1 tsp honey

Directions

1. In a bowl, mix together all the ingredients.
2. Serve immediately or this relish can be served chilled.

Quesadillas
Martinique

Prep Time: 10 mins
Total Time: 30 mins

Servings per Recipe: 6
Calories	503 kcal
Fat	24.2 g
Carbohydrates	49.2g
Protein	23.2 g
Cholesterol	39 mg
Sodium	1421 mg

Ingredients

1 (15 oz.) can black beans, drained
1 tbsp vegetable oil
1/2 onion, chopped
1 red bell pepper, chopped
1 tsp chili powder
1 pinch cayenne pepper
1 pinch dried oregano
1 pinch dried basil
1 mango - peeled, seeded and diced

1 (6 oz.) package seasoned chicken-style vegetarian strips
6 (10 inch) flour tortillas
1 (8 oz.) package shredded Cheddar cheese
1 C. arugula leaves
1 (4 oz.) jar jalapeno pepper rings
1 (8 oz.) jar salsa

Directions

1. In a pan, add the beans on medium heat and cook for about 5 minutes.
2. With a potato masher, mash them partially. Reduce the heat to very low to keep warm till serving.
3. In a large skillet, heat the oil on medium heat and sauté the onion and bell pepper, herbs, cayenne pepper and chili powder till vegetables become tender.
4. Stir in the vegetarian strips and mango and cook for about 2 minutes.
5. Meanwhile heat another skillet on medium heat and cook the tortillas, one at a time and cook for about 2 minutes per side.
6. Arrange the tortillas onto smooth surface and top with the beans, followed by the mango mixture, Cheddar cheese, arugula, and jalapenos.
7. Fold tortillas over the filling and serve with a topping of the salsa.

WEST INDIAN INSPIRED
Guacamole

🍲 Prep Time: 20 mins
🕐 Total Time: 20 mins

Servings per Recipe: 8
Calories	198 kcal
Fat	14.9 g
Cholesterol	19g
Sodium	2.5 g
Carbohydrates	0 mg
Protein	49 mg

Ingredients

2 tbsp minced white onion
2 limes, juiced
2 serrano chili peppers
2 limes, juiced
sea salt to taste

4 ripe avocados, peeled and pitted
1/4 C. chopped fresh cilantro
1 large mango - peeled, seeded, and chopped

Directions

1. In a bowl, mix together the juice of the 2 limes and onion and keep aside for about 1 hour.
2. Strain well and squeezes to remove the extra juice, then keep aside.
3. In a food processor, add the juice of the 2 limes, Serrano Chili and salt and pulse till chopped finely.
4. Add the avocado and pulse till smooth.
5. Transfer the mixture into a serving bowl.
6. Add the onion, mango and cilantro and stir to combine.
7. Serve immediately.

May Pen
Ceviche

 Prep Time: 20 mins
 Total Time: 1 hr 20 mins

Servings per Recipe: 6
Calories	80 kcal
Fat	0.4 g
Cholesterol	20.1g
Sodium	1.4 g
Carbohydrates	0 mg
Protein	7 mg

Ingredients

3 mangos - peeled, seeded, and diced
1 yellow onion, diced
1 green bell pepper, diced
1 red bell pepper, diced
3 jalapeno peppers, minced

1/2 bunch fresh cilantro, minced
2 limes, juiced (with pulp)

Directions

1. In a bowl, mix together all the ingredients.
2. Refrigerate, covered for about 1 hour.

HOW TO MAKE
a Mango Pie

🥣 Prep Time: 20 mins

🕐 Total Time: 1 hr 20 mins

Servings per Recipe: 8	
Calories	549 kcal
Fat	22.6 g
Carbohydrates	86.6g
Protein	4.7 g
Cholesterol	15 mg
Sodium	371 mg

Ingredients

8 extra green mangoes, peeled, seeded, and sliced
1 tbsp lime juice
1 C. white sugar
1/3 C. all-purpose flour
1/4 tsp salt

1/2 tsp ground allspice
1 (15 oz.) package prepared double pie crust
1/4 C. butter

Directions

1. Set your oven to 350 degrees F before doing anything else.
2. In a bowl, add the mangoes and lime juice and toss to coat well.
3. In another bowl, mix together the flour, sugar, allspice and salt.
4. In the bottom of the pie shell, place the sugar mixture and the sliced mangoes in several layers.
5. Place the butter on the top in the shape of the dots and top with the other half of the pie crust.
6. With a fork, prick the top and cook everything in the oven for about 1 hour.

Monica's
Mango Glaze

Prep Time: 10 mins
Total Time: 25 mins

Servings per Recipe: 4
Calories	120 kcal
Fat	3.2 g
Carbohydrates	24.6 g
Protein	0.7 g
Cholesterol	8 mg
Sodium	24 mg

Ingredients

3 C. mangos, peeled, seeded and chopped
1 tbsp butter
1 tbsp brown sugar
1 tsp lemon juice
1 tsp orange juice

3 tbsp water

Directions

1. In a pan, add all the ingredients on medium heat and cook stirring till the mixture becomes thick.
2. Remove everything from the heat and serve.

3-INGREDIENT
Mango Juice

🥣 Prep Time: 10 mins
🕐 Total Time: 10 mins

Servings per Recipe: 2
Calories	226 kcal
Fat	0.9 g
Cholesterol	61.3g
Sodium	1.9 g
Carbohydrates	0 mg
Protein	7 mg

Ingredients

2 medium mangos, peeled and sliced
2 peeled limes
2 apples, cored and quartered

Directions

1. In a juicer, add all the ingredients and process according to manufacturer's directions.
2. Serve over the ice cubes.

Island
Gazpacho

Prep Time: 20 mins
Total Time: 20 mins

Servings per Recipe: 6
Calories	147 kcal
Fat	5 g
Cholesterol	26.2g
Sodium	1.6 g
Carbohydrates	0 mg
Protein	5 mg

Ingredients

2 C. 1/4-inch-diced fresh mangoes
2 C. orange juice
2 tbsp extra-virgin olive oil
1 seedless cucumber, cut into 1/4-inch dice
1 small red bell pepper, seeded and cut into 1/4-inch dice
1 small onion, cut into 1/4-inch dice
2 medium garlic cloves, minced

1 small jalapeno pepper, seeded and minced
3 tbsp fresh lime juice
2 tbsp chopped fresh parsley
Salt and freshly ground black pepper

Directions

1. In a blender, add the mangoes, oil and orange juice and pulse till pureed.
2. Transfer the mango puree in a bowl with the remaining all ingredients and mix well.
3. Refrigerate till serving.

2-INGREDIENT
Mango Mousse

🥣 Prep Time: 15 mins

🕐 Total Time: 3 hrs 15 mins

Servings per Recipe: 4

Calories	232 kcal
Fat	22.1 g
Cholesterol	8.7g
Sodium	1.4 g
Carbohydrates	82 mg
Protein	23 mg

Ingredients

1 C. heavy whipping cream
1 C. mango, pureed

Directions

1. In a glass bowl, add the cream and beat till stiff peaks form.
2. The whipped cream will form sharp peaks by lifting the beater straight up.
3. Fold in the mango puree and transfer into serving glasses.
4. Refrigerate to chill for about 3 hours.

Mango
Bars

🥣 Prep Time: 20 mins
🕐 Total Time: 1 hr 15 mins

Servings per Recipe: 12	
Calories	277 kcal
Fat	12.1 g
Carbohydrates	40.2g
Protein	3.6 g
Cholesterol	51 mg
Sodium	141 mg

Ingredients

3/4 C. chopped dried mango
1 C. all-purpose flour
1/4 C. confectioners' sugar
1/2 C. butter
1 C. packed brown sugar
1/3 C. all-purpose flour
2 eggs, beaten

1/2 C. chopped mixed nuts
1/2 tsp baking powder
1/4 tsp lemon extract
1/4 tsp salt
confectioners' sugar for dusting

Directions

1. Set your oven to 350 degrees F before doing anything else and line a 9x9-inch baking pan with wax paper.
2. In a medium pan, add the mango and enough water to cover on low heat and cook for about 15 minutes. Remove everything from the heat and drain, then keep aside.
3. In a large bowl, mix together 1 C. of the flour and 1/4 C. of the confectioners' sugar.
4. With a pastry cutter, cut the butter and mix till a coarse crumbs form.
5. Place the mixture into the prepared baking pan to make a crust.
6. Cook everything in the oven for about 10 minutes. In a bowl, add the mango, eggs, mixed nuts, brown sugar, 1/3 C. of the flour, baking powder, lemon extract and salt and mix till well combined.
7. Transfer the mixture over the prepared crust evenly.Cover, and cook everything in the oven for about 20 minutes. Remove everything from the oven and keep aside to cool slightly.
8. Serve with a dusting of the confectioners' sugar.

KINGSTON CITY
Frappe

🥣 Prep Time: 5 mins

🕐 Total Time: 10 mins

Servings per Recipe: 3

Calories	78 kcal
Fat	0.3 g
Carbohydrates	19.9g
Protein	0.9 g
Cholesterol	0 mg
Sodium	6 mg

Ingredients

1 mango - peeled, seeded, and cut into chunks
3/4 C. orange juice
1/4 C. lime juice

2 ice cubes
1 1/4 C. club soda

Directions

1. In a blender, add the mango and pulse till a smooth puree forms.
2. Add both the juices and pulse till smooth.
3. Add the club soda and ice cubes and pulse till the ice cubes are crushed.

Caribbean
Bruschetta

🥣 Prep Time: 15 mins
🕐 Total Time: 25 mins

Servings per Recipe: 6
Calories   315 kcal
Fat   6.8 g
Carbohydrates   48.7g
Protein   15.3 g
Cholesterol   21 mg
Sodium   724 mg

Ingredients

1 (1 lb.) loaf French bread, cut into 1/2 inch pieces
1 mango - peeled, seeded and diced
1 tbsp fresh basil, minced

1 C. grated Romano cheese

Directions

1. Set your oven to the broiler.
2. In a large baking sheet, place the French bread slices in a single layer and cook under the broiler for about 1-2 minutes per side.
3. Remove everything from the oven.
4. Ina bowl, mix together the basil and mango and spread the mixture over each bread slice.
5. Top with the Romano cheese and cook under the broiler for about 2-3 minutes.
6. Serve hot.

CHILIAD
Mango

🥣 Prep Time: 5 mins
🕐 Total Time: 15 mins

Servings per Recipe: 2
Calories	85 kcal
Fat	0.9 g
Carbohydrates	21.7g
Protein	1.1 g
Cholesterol	0 mg
Sodium	237 mg

Ingredients

1/4 C. water
1 tbsp chili powder
1 pinch salt

3 tbsp lemon juice
1 mango - peeled, seeded, and sliced

Directions

1. In a small pan, add the water and bring to a boil.
2. Add the lemon juice, chili powder and salt and cook, stirring till heated through.
3. Stir in the mango and toss to coat well.
4. Remove everything from the heat and keep aside for a few minutes before serving.

How to Make
a Mango Cake

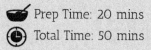 Prep Time: 20 mins

Total Time: 50 mins

Servings per Recipe: 12
Calories	274 kcal
Fat	14.6 g
Cholesterol	32.7g
Sodium	4.3 g
Carbohydrates	59 mg
Protein	211 mg

Ingredients

1 1/2 C. all-purpose flour
1 tsp baking soda
2/3 C. butter
1 C. white sugar
2 eggs
1 C. buttermilk

1 tsp vanilla extract
1 C. mango puree
1/2 C. chopped walnuts

Directions

1. Set your oven to 375 degrees F before doing anything else and grease a 9x5-inch loaf pan.
2. In a bowl, add the sugar and butter and beat till fluffy.
3. Add the eggs and beat well.
4. In another bowl, mix together the flour and baking soda.
5. Add the flour mixture into the egg mixture and mix well.
6. Fold in the remaining ingredients.
7. Transfer the mixture into the prepared loaf pan and cook everything in the oven for about 40-50 minutes.

SWEET HONEY
Butter

Prep Time: 10 mins

Total Time: 10 mins

Servings per Recipe: 8

Calories	119 kcal
Fat	5.8 g
Cholesterol	18.3g
Sodium	0.2 g
Carbohydrates	15 mg
Protein	42 mg

Ingredients

1/2 C. honey
1/4 C. softened butter
1/4 C. finely chopped mango

Directions

1. In a bowl, add all the ingredients and bet till well combined.

Jamaican
Mango Chicken

🥄 Prep Time: 20 mins
🕐 Total Time: 30 mins

Servings per Recipe: 4
Calories	312 kcal
Fat	5.4 g
Cholesterol	36.4g
Sodium	29.2 g
Carbohydrates	68 mg
Protein	81 mg

Ingredients

4 skinless, boneless chicken breasts
3/4 C. chopped red onion
1 mango - peeled, seeded, and sliced
1 tbsp vegetable oil
3 C. orange juice

3 tbsp cornstarch
1/4 C. hot water

Directions

1. Heat a large skillet and cook the chicken till browned completely.
2. Add the red onion and cook, stirring occasionally for about 2-3 minutes.
3. Stir in the orange juice and bring to a boil.
4. Stir in the mango slices and reduce the heat, then simmer for about 2 minutes.
5. Meanwhile in a bowl, mix together the hot water and cornstarch.
6. Add the cornstarch mixture in the pan and cook, stirring till the mixture becomes thick.

CROP-OVER
Smoothies

🍽 Prep Time: 10 mins
🕐 Total Time: 10 mins

Servings per Recipe: 2
Calories	105 kcal
Fat	1.3 g
Cholesterol	22.3g
Sodium	2.5 g
Carbohydrates	0 mg
Protein	29 mg

Ingredients

1 peach, sliced
1 mango, peeled and diced
1/2 C. vanilla soy milk

1/2 C. orange juice, or as needed

Directions

1. In a blender, add all the ingredients and pulse till smooth.
2. Transfer into glasses and serve.

Mango
Lunch Box Salad

Prep Time: 15 mins
Total Time: 15 mins

Servings per Recipe: 12

Calories	319 kcal
Fat	20.2 g
Cholesterol	34.2g
Sodium	3.4 g
Carbohydrates	0 mg
Protein	205 mg

Ingredients

1/2 C. sugar
3/4 C. canola oil
1 tsp salt
1/4 C. balsamic vinegar
8 C. mixed salad greens
2 C. sweetened dried cranberries
1/2 lb. fresh strawberries, quartered

1 mango - peeled, seeded, and cubed
1/2 C. chopped onion
1 C. slivered almonds

Directions

1. In a small bowl, add the sugar, salt, oil and vinegar and beat well.
2. In a serving bowl, mix together all the ingredients except the almonds.
3. Pour the vinaigrette and toss to coat well.
4. Serve with a topping of the almonds.

KERALA
Sweet Smoothies

🥘 Prep Time: 5 mins
🕐 Total Time: 5 mins

Servings per Recipe: 2
Calories   482 kcal
Fat   4.4 g
Cholesterol   102.4g
Sodium   13.9 g
Carbohydrates   15 mg
Protein   179 mg

Ingredients

2 mangos - peeled, seeded and diced
2 C. plain yogurt
1/2 C. white sugar

1 C. ice

Directions

1. In a blender, add all the ingredients and pulse till smooth.
2. Transfer into glasses and serve.

Spicy Tilapia
with Mango Chutney

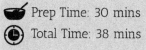

Prep Time: 30 mins
Total Time: 38 mins

Servings per Recipe: 4
Calories	211 kcal
Fat	8.7 g
Carbohydrates	9.5g
Protein	23.7 g
Cholesterol	41 mg
Sodium	691 mg

Ingredients

1 mango - peeled and diced
1/4 C. chopped red onion
1 serrano chili, minced
1/2 C. cilantro leaves, chopped
2 tbsp lime juice
1/2 tsp salt
2 tbsp olive oil, divided

1 tbsp curry powder
1 tbsp garlic pepper seasoning
4 fresh tilapia fillets

Directions

1. For the mango salsa, in a bowl, mix together the mango, red onion, Serrano chili, cilantro, lime juice and salt.
2. Rub the tilapia fillets with the garlic pepper and curry powder evenly.
3. Drizzle with 1 tbsp of the oil.
4. In a large skillet, heat the remaining oil on medium-high heat sear the fish fillets for about 3 minutes per side.
5. Serve the tilapia fillets with a topping of the mango salsa.

AFTER-SCHOOL
Smoothie

🍳 Prep Time: 5 mins

🕐 Total Time: 5 mins

Servings per Recipe: 2

Calories	135 kcal
Fat	0.9 g
Cholesterol	30.4g
Sodium	3.2 g
Carbohydrates	2 mg
Protein	39 mg

Ingredients

1 banana
1/2 C. frozen mango pieces
1/3 C. plain yogurt

1/2 C. orange-mango juice blend

Directions

1. In a blender, add all the ingredients and pulse till smooth.

Coconut
Mango Muffins

Prep Time: 20 mins
Total Time: 45 mins

Servings per Recipe: 16
Calories	219 kcal
Fat	8.4 g
Carbohydrates	33.9g
Protein	3.1 g
Cholesterol	43 mg
Sodium	165 mg

Ingredients

1/4 C. all-purpose flour
1/4 tsp ground cinnamon
1 tbsp white sugar
3 tbsp sweetened flaked coconut, chopped
1 pinch salt
2 tbsp butter
1/2 C. unsalted butter
1 1/4 C. white sugar
1/2 tsp salt
2 eggs
1 3/4 C. all-purpose flour

2 tsp baking powder
1/2 C. buttermilk
1 C. fresh blueberries
1/4 C. all-purpose flour
1 C. mango - peeled, seeded and diced

Directions

1. Set your oven to 375 degrees F before doing anything else and grease 16 cups of the muffin tins.
2. In a bowl, mix together the 1/4 C. of the flour, cinnamon, 1 tbsp of the sugar, coconut, and 1 pinch of the salt.
3. Add 2 tbsp of the butter and mix till well combined.
4. In a second bowl, add the unsalted butter, 1 1/4 C. of the sugar, and 1/2 tsp of the salt and beat till smooth.
5. Add the eggs, one at a time, beating continuously till fluffy.
6. In a third bowl, mix together the 1 3/4 C. of the flour and baking powder.
7. Add the flour mixture into the butter mixture alternately with the buttermilk and mix well.

8. In a small bowl, add the blueberries and 1/4 C. of the flour and toss to coat well.
9. Add the blueberry mixture and mango in the flour mixture and mix.
10. Transfer the mixture into the prepared muffin cups and sprinkle with the coconut mixture.
11. Cook everything in the oven for about 25-35 minutes.

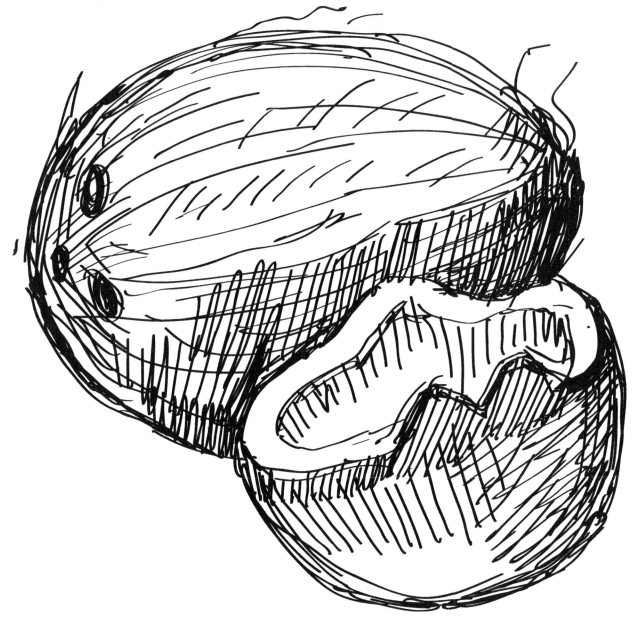

Fruity
Quinoa Salad

 Prep Time: 10 mins
Total Time: 1 hr 25 mins

Servings per Recipe: 4
Calories	162 kcal
Fat	2.4 g
Carbohydrates	31.1g
Protein	5.3 g
Cholesterol	1 mg
Sodium	553 mg

Ingredients

1 1/2 C. chicken stock
3/4 C. quinoa
1 1/2 tsp curry powder
1/4 tsp garlic powder
1/2 tsp salt

1/4 tsp black pepper
1 mango - peeled, seeded and diced
3 green onions, chopped

Directions

1. In a pan, mix together the chicken broth, quinoa, curry powder, garlic powder, salt, and black pepper and bring to a boil on high heat.
2. Reduce the heat to medium-low and simmer, covered until for about 15-20 minutes.
3. Transfer the quinoa into a shallow dish and keep aside to cool.
4. Stir in the mango and green onions and serve

TROPICAL
Cheesecake

Prep Time: 35 mins

Total Time: 9 hrs 30 mins

Servings per Recipe: 8
Calories	468 kcal
Fat	31.6 g
Carbohydrates	38.4g
Protein	9.4 g
Cholesterol	131 mg
Sodium	311 mg

Ingredients

3/4 C. sweetened flaked coconut
3/4 C. crushed gingersnap cookies
3 tbsp melted butter
2 (8 oz.) packages cream cheese, softened
1 (10 oz.) can sweetened condensed milk
2 eggs
1 tbsp lime zest

2 tbsp lime juice
1 tbsp coconut extract
2 C. cubed fresh mango
1 tsp white sugar

Directions

1. Set your oven to 325 degrees F before doing anything else and lightly, grease a 9 - inch spring form pan.
2. Transfer the mixture into the bottom and slightly up the sides of the prepared pan.
3. Cook everything in the oven for about 10 minutes.
4. Remove everything from the oven and keep aside to cool.
5. Now, set your oven to 300 degrees F.
6. In a bowl, add the softened cream cheese and beat till smooth.
7. With beater set to medium - low, slowly add the condensed milk into the bowl, mixing till well combined. Add the eggs, one at a time, beating continuously till well combined.
8. Transfer about half of the cream cheese mixture into another bowl.
9. Add the lime juice and lime zest into the portion in another bowl and place the mixture over the crust evenly.

36   Tropical Cheesecake

10. Stir the coconut extract in the remaining cream cheese mixture and place over the lime-flavored batter cream cheese mixture evenly.
11. Cook everything in the oven for about 45 minutes.
12. Turn the heat of the oven off, but keep the cheesecake inside with oven door slightly open till the oven cools completely.
13. Refrigerate the cheesecake till chilled completely.
14. For mango coulis in a blender, add the mango and sugar and pulse till smooth.
15. Drizzle over cheesecake just before serving.

Dinner (Chicken and Fruity Rice)

🥣 Prep Time: 15 mins
🕐 Total Time: 45 mins

Servings per Recipe: 4
Calories	379 kcal
Fat	3 g
Carbohydrates	53.8g
Protein	27.1 g
Cholesterol	61 mg
Sodium	347 mg

Ingredients

1 tsp curry powder
1/2 tsp salt
1/4 tsp black pepper
4 skinless, boneless chicken breast halves
1 C. chicken broth
1/2 C. water
1/2 C. apple juice

1 C. long-grain white rice
1 tbsp brown sugar
1 tbsp dried parsley
1 C. diced mango

Directions

1. In a bowl, mix together the curry powder, 1/4 tsp of the salt and black pepper.
2. Add the chicken pieces and coat with the mixture generously.
3. In a nonstick skillet, mix together the rice, apple juice, broth and water.
4. Stir in the remaining 1/4 tsp of the salt and all the ingredients and place the chicken pieces on the top, then bring to a boil.
5. Reduce the heat to low and simmer, covered for about 20-25 minutes.
6. Remove everything from the heat and keep aside covered for about 5 minutes before serving.

Breaded
Mango Pudding

Prep Time: 15 mins
Total Time: 1 hr

Servings per Recipe: 8
Calories	194 kcal
Fat	6.7 g
Carbohydrates	27.9 g
Protein	6.1 g
Cholesterol	82 mg
Sodium	201 mg

Ingredients

6 slices white bread, torn into small pieces
2 mangos - peeled, seeded and diced
1/4 C. white sugar
3 eggs, lightly beaten
2 C. milk

1 1/2 tsp vanilla extract
1 1/2 tsp ground cardamom
2 tbsp butter

Directions

1. Set your oven to 350 degrees F before doing anything else and grease an 11x9-inch baking dish.
2. In a bowl, add the mango and bread pieces and toss to coat and transfer into the prepared baking dish.
3. In a bowl, add the milk, eggs, sugar, cardamom and vanilla and beat till well combined.
4. Place the egg mixture over the mango mixture and cook everything in the oven for about 45-50 minutes.

MANGO
Chutney Bites

🥣 Prep Time: 15 mins
🕐 Total Time: 3 hrs 15 mins

Servings per Recipe: 6

Calories	465 kcal
Fat	28.5 g
Cholesterol	47.9 g
Sodium	9.6 g
Carbohydrates	71 mg
Protein	854 mg

Ingredients

11 oz. cream cheese, at room temperature
1 C. golden raisins
1 (2.1 oz.) package cooked turkey bacon, diced
1 bunch green onions, chopped

3 tbsp sour cream
1 (9 oz.) jar mango chutney

Directions

1. In a bowl, add the cream cheese, sour cream, bacon, raisins and green onions and mix till well combined.
2. Make a ball from the mixture and cover with a plastic wrap.
3. Refrigerate for at least 3 hours or overnight before serving.
4. Place the cheese ball on a serving platter and top with the mango chutney.
5. Serve alongside the crackers for dipping.

Saint George
Salmon

Prep Time: 15 mins
Total Time: 45 mins

Servings per Recipe: 4
Calories	438 kcal
Fat	28.2 g
Carbohydrates	17.7g
Protein	29 g
Cholesterol	98 mg
Sodium	255 mg

Ingredients

2 tbsp olive oil
4 (4 oz.) fillets salmon
4 oz. Brie cheese, sliced
1 tsp butter

2 mangos - peeled, seeded, and diced

Directions

1. Set your oven to 350 degrees F before doing anything else.
2. In a large oven proof skillet, heat the oil on medium-high heat and sear the salmon for about 4 minutes per side.
3. Place the cheese over the salmon fillets evenly.
4. Cover the skillet and transfer into the oven.
5. Cook everything in the oven for about 15 minutes.
6. Meanwhile in a pan, melt the butter on medium heat and cook the mangoes for about 15 minutes.
7. Serve the salmon with a topping of the cooked mango.

4-INGREDIENT
Cold Mango Soup

Prep Time: 10 mins
Total Time: 10 mins

Servings per Recipe: 3

Calories	319 kcal
Fat	14.4 g
Cholesterol	49.2g
Sodium	4.7 g
Carbohydrates	45 mg
Protein	53 mg

Ingredients

2 mango - peeled, seeded, and cubed
1/4 C. white sugar
1 lemon, zested and juiced

1 1/2 C. half-and-half

Directions

1. In a blender, add all the ingredients and pulse till smooth.
2. Serve chilled.

Tropical
Shortbread

 Prep Time: 15 mins

Total Time: 1 hr 30 mins

Servings per Recipe: 20
Calories	247 kcal
Fat	14.1 g
Carbohydrates	28.8g
Protein	2.4 g
Cholesterol	37 mg
Sodium	99 mg

Ingredients

1 1/2 C. butter
1/2 C. white sugar
3 C. sifted all-purpose flour
4 C. sliced mango
1/4 C. white sugar

1/4 C. all-purpose flour
1 1/2 tsp ground cinnamon
1 pinch ground allspice

Directions

1. Set your oven to 350 degrees F before doing anything else.
2. In a large bowl, add the 1/2 C. of the sugar and butter and beat till creamy.
3. Add the 3 C. of the flour and mix till well combined.
4. In the bottom of a 13x9-inch baking dish, place half of of the flour mixture and press to smooth.
5. In another bowl, mix together the remaining ingredients and place over the flour mixture evenly.
6. Top with the remaining flour mixture and cook everything in the oven for about 1 hour.

TRINIDAD
Spicy Mangoes

🥘 Prep Time: 25 mins

🕐 Total Time: 45 mins

Servings per Recipe: 4	
Calories	323 kcal
Fat	21.6 g
Carbohydrates	19.1g
Protein	17.7 g
Cholesterol	0 mg
Sodium	175 mg

Ingredients

1 tbsp sesame oil
5 cloves garlic, minced
1 tbsp minced ginger
1 firm mango, peeled and sliced
3 tbsp yellow curry powder

2 tbsp chopped cilantro
1 (14 oz.) can light coconut milk
1 (14 oz.) package extra firm tofu, cubed
1/4 tsp salt and pepper to taste

Directions

1. In a large skillet, heat the oil on medium-high heat and sauté the ginger and garlic for about 1-2 minutes.
2. Add the mango and cook for about 1 minute.
3. Stir in the cilantro and curry powder and cook for about 1 minute.
4. Stir in the coconut milk and bring to a simmer.
5. Stir in the tofu, salt and black pepper and simmer, stirring occasionally for about 5 minutes.

Caribbean
Lassi

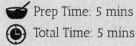 Prep Time: 5 mins
Total Time: 5 mins

Servings per Recipe: 4
Calories	121 kcal
Fat	1.2 g
Cholesterol	27.8g
Sodium	2.3 g
Carbohydrates	3 mg
Protein	50 mg

Ingredients

2 (15.25 oz.) cans mango pulp, or mango slices with juice
1/2 C. plain yogurt

1/4 C. milk
2 C. ice cubes

Directions

1. In a blender, add all the ingredients and pulse till smooth.

TROPICAL
Coleslaw

🥣 Prep Time: 20 mins

🕐 Total Time: 40 mins

Servings per Recipe: 8

Calories	81 kcal
Fat	5 g
Cholesterol	9.1g
Sodium	1.8 g
Carbohydrates	0 mg
Protein	7 mg

Ingredients

4 C. shredded cabbage
1/2 C. finely chopped red onion
1 fresh mango, cubed
1/2 C. walnut pieces
1/4 C. SPLENDA(R) Granular

3/4 C. white rice vinegar

Directions

1. In a bowl, mix together the cabbage, mango, onion and walnut.
2. In another small bowl, mix together the Splenda and vinegar.
3. Pour over the salad and toss to coat well.
4. Serve immediately or it can be served chilled too.

Mango
Blender

Prep Time: 10 mins
Total Time: 10 mins

Servings per Recipe: 2
Calories   255 kcal
Fat   3.9 g
Cholesterol   52.1g
Sodium   6.7 g
Carbohydrates   15 mg
Protein   82 mg

Ingredients

1 mango - peeled, seeded and diced
1 1/2 C. milk
3 tbsp honey

1 C. ice cubes

Directions

1. In a blender, add all the ingredients and pulse till smooth.
2. Serve immediately.

TROPICAL
Lassi

Prep Time: 15 mins
Total Time: 15 mins

Servings per Recipe: 3
Calories	228 kcal
Fat	3 g
Cholesterol	43.6g
Sodium	9.4 g
Carbohydrates	10 mg
Protein	121 mg

Ingredients

1 large mango - peeled, seeded, and diced
3 tbsp brown sugar
2 tbsp chopped fresh mint
1 tsp freshly ground star anise
1 tsp freshly ground cardamom

1 tbsp lime juice
2 C. plain yogurt
3 sprigs fresh mint for garnish

Directions

1. In a blender, add all the ingredients except the mint and pulse till smooth.
2. Transfer into the glasses and serve with a garnishing of the mint leaves.

Peach Nectarine
Smoothie

Prep Time: 5 mins
Total Time: 5 mins

Servings per Recipe: 4
Calories	150 kcal
Fat	0.6 g
Cholesterol	38.4g
Sodium	1.3 g
Carbohydrates	0 mg
Protein	9 mg

Ingredients

3 C. diced mango
1 1/2 C. chopped fresh or frozen peaches
1/4 C. chopped orange segments
1/4 C. chopped and pitted nectarine
1/2 C. orange juice

2 C. ice

Directions

1. In a blender, add all the ingredients and pulse till smooth.

MANGO DRINK
Chinese Style

Prep Time: 10 mins
Total Time: 50 mins

Servings per Recipe: 2
Calories   315 kcal
Fat   12.3 g
Carbohydrates   52.9g
Protein   1.7 g
Cholesterol   0 mg
Sodium   14 mg

Ingredients

1/2 C. small pearl tapioca
1 mango - peeled, seeded and diced
14 ice cubes

1/2 C. coconut milk

Directions

1. In a pan of boiling water, cook the tapioca pearls for about 10 minutes, stirring occasionally.
2. Cover and remove everything from the heat, then keep aside for about 30 minutes.
3. Drain well and refrigerate, covered before serving.
4. In a blender, add the mango and ice and pulse till smooth.
5. Divide the chilled tapioca pearls in 2 tall glasses and top with the mango mixture, followed by the coconut milk.

Homemade
Fruit Punch

Prep Time: 10 mins
Total Time: 10 mins

Servings per Recipe: 8
Calories	61 kcal
Fat	0.1 g
Cholesterol	15.4g
Sodium	0.5 g
Carbohydrates	0 mg
Protein	5 mg

Ingredients

1 C. sliced mango
1 C. diced, peeled papaya
1 C. orange juice
1/4 C. lime juice
1/4 C. white sugar, or to taste

1 tsp grated orange zest
4 C. water

Directions

1. In a blender, add the papaya and mango and pulse till smooth.
2. Add the remaining ingredients and pulse till well combined.
3. Serve immediately over the crushed ice.

SIESTA KEY
Honey Smoothie

Prep Time: 10 mins
Total Time: 10 mins

Servings per Recipe: 2

Calories	198 kcal
Fat	0.4 g
Cholesterol	47.5g
Sodium	4.7 g
Carbohydrates	2 mg
Protein	58 mg

Ingredients

1 mango - peeled, seeded and cubed
1 tbsp white sugar
2 tbsp honey
1 C. nonfat milk

1 tsp lemon juice
1 C. ice cubes

Directions

1. In a blender, add all the ingredients and pulse till smooth.
2. Divide the ice cubes in two serving glasses.
3. Add the mango smoothie over ice and serve.

Tropical
Mango Pie

🥣 Prep Time: 15 mins
🕐 Total Time: 2 hrs 20 mins

Servings per Recipe: 24
Calories   219 kcal
Fat   11.7 g
Carbohydrates   27.1g
Protein   2.5 g
Cholesterol   26 mg
Sodium   101 mg

Ingredients

2 C. all-purpose flour, sifted
1/2 C. confectioners' sugar
3/4 C. butter
1 (8 oz.) package cream cheese, softened
1/2 C. white sugar
1 tsp vanilla extract
3/4 (12 oz.) container whipped topping
1 C. cold water

2 envelopes unflavored beef gelatin
1 C. boiling water
1/2 C. white sugar
1/4 tsp salt
1/4 C. lemon juice
5 C. diced mango

Directions

1. Set your oven to 350 degrees F before doing anything else.
2. In a bowl, mix together the flour and confectioners' sugar.
3. With a pastry cutter, cut the butter and mix till a coarse crumb forms.
4. Transfer the mixture into a 13x9-inch baking dish and cook everything in the oven for about 20-25 minutes.
5. Remove everything from the oven and keep aside to cool completely.
6. In a bowl, add the cream cheese, 1/2 C. of the white sugar, and vanilla extract and beat till smooth.
7. Fold in the whipped topping and place the mixture over the crust evenly.
8. Refrigerate for about 30 minutes.
9. In a bowl, add the cold water and sprinkle with the gelatin, then stir well.
10. Place the hot water over gelatin mixture and stir till the gelatin dissolves completely.

11. Add 1/2 C. of the sugar and salt into gelatin mixture and stir till the sugar dissolves.
12. Add the lemon juice and keep aside to cool.
13. Fold in the mango and refrigerate for about 15-20 minutes.
14. Pour mango gelatin over cream cheese filling and refrigerate for about 1 hour.

Mango Cobbler

🥣 Prep Time: 15 mins
🕐 Total Time: 1 hr

Servings per Recipe: 12
Calories	384 kcal
Fat	8.5 g
Carbohydrates	76.1g
Protein	3.4 g
Cholesterol	22 mg
Sodium	277 mg

Ingredients

Mangos:
8 mangoes - peeled, seeded, and sliced
2 C. water
1/2 C. white sugar
Batter:
2 C. white sugar
1/2 C. butter, softened

2 C. all-purpose flour
4 tsp baking powder
1/4 tsp salt
1 C. milk
1 tbsp vanilla extract

Directions

1. Set your oven to 375 degrees F before doing anything else.
2. In a pan, mix together the mangoes, 1/2 C. of the sugar and water on medium heat and simmer for about 5-6 minutes, stirring occasionally.
3. Drain the syrup from the mangoes, reserving in a bowl.
4. In a bowl, add the butter and 2 C. of the sugar and beat till creamy.
5. In another bowl mix together the flour, baking powder and salt.
6. Slowly, add the flour mixture and milk into the butter mixture and mix well.
7. Add the vanilla extract and mix till well combined.
8. Transfer the mixture into a 13x9-inch baking dish evenly and top with the mango slices.
9. Place bout 2 C. of the reserved syrup over the mangoes evenly and cook everything in the oven for about 40-45 minutes.

CARIBBEAN
Fluff

🥣 Prep Time: 10 mins
🕐 Total Time: 10 mins

Servings per Recipe: 8
Calories	192 kcal
Fat	11.4 g
Cholesterol	23.6g
Sodium	1.6 g
Carbohydrates	41 mg
Protein	13 mg

Ingredients

1 C. heavy whipping cream
1 tsp vanilla extract
2 ripe mangoes, peeled and chopped
3 bananas, thickly sliced

2 (6 oz.) containers fresh blueberries

Directions

1. In a bowl, add the cream and vanilla extract and beat till stiff peaks form.
2. The whipped cream will form sharp peaks by lifting the beater straight up.
3. Gently. Fold in the fruit

Printed in Great Britain
by Amazon

31623885R00033